POEMS BY

SUSAN WOOD

# CAMPO SANTO

LOUISIANA STATE UNIVERSITY PRESS

BATON ROUGE AND LONDON

1991

FIRST PRINTING
00  99  98  97  96  95  94  93  92  91    5  4  3  2  1

DESIGNER: AMANDA MCDONALD KEY
TYPEFACE: BEMBO
TYPESETTER: G&S TYPESETTERS, INC.
PRINTER AND BINDER: THOMSON-SHORE, INC.

LIBRARY OF CONGRESS CATALOGING-IN-PUBLICATION DATA

WOOD, SUSAN, 1946–
  CAMPO SANTO : POEMS / BY SUSAN WOOD.
    P.    CM.
  ISBN 0-8071-1676-9 (CLOTH : ALK. PAPER). — ISBN 0-8071-1677-7
(PAPER : ALK. PAPER)
  I. TITLE.
PS3573.O597C36  1991
811'.54—DC20                91-9863
                               CIP

THE AUTHOR OFFERS GRATEFUL ACKNOWLEDGMENT TO THE EDITORS OF THE FOLLOWING
PERIODICALS, IN WHICH MANY OF THE POEMS HEREIN FIRST APPEARED: *ANTIOCH REVIEW, GULF
COAST, INDIANA REVIEW, MISSOURI REVIEW, NEW ENGLAND REVIEW AND BREAD LOAF
QUARTERLY, SEATTLE REVIEW, SLANT, TAMPA REVIEW,* AND *TENDRIL.* "DISTANCES," "LATE-
BLOOMERS," "EGGS," "SUNDAY NIGHTS," AND "ON FIRE" WERE FIRST PUBLISHED IN *POETRY.*
"FOURTH OF JULY, TEXAS, 1956" AND "PINK VISTA" FIRST APPEARED IN *PLOUGHSHARES.*

THE PAPER IN THIS BOOK MEETS THE GUIDELINES FOR PERMANENCE AND DURABILITY OF THE
COMMITTEE ON PRODUCTION GUIDELINES FOR BOOK LONGEVITY OF THE COUNCIL ON LIBRARY
RESOURCES. ∞

# Campo Santo

*Campo Santo* is the 1991 Lamont Poetry Selection
of The Academy of American Poets.

From 1954 through 1974 the Lamont Poetry Selection
supported the publication and distribution of a first
collection of poems. Since 1975 this distinguished
award has been given for an American poet's second book.

Judges for 1991: Marvin Bell, Robert Morgan, and
Lucille Clifton.

To the memory of my mother.
Martha Jo Lee McDowell, 1917–1987

*Between grief and nothing, I will take grief.*
—William Faulkner, *The Wild Palms*

# Contents

# HILLS ABOVE HALF MOON BAY

Often, those first mornings, pale disc
of a moon still hanging in the deep blue
folds of sky, you'd walk out along the hills
to watch the light not fall, exactly, but gather,
as though someone were slowly raising a curtain.
Beyond the foothills the Pacific floated
in the clouds and, looking out, you thought
the hills themselves seemed artificial, a painting's
stylized idea, the way experience seen
from a great distance seems somehow
unreal, and more intense. Once a man told you
he wanted only plains, a flat expansiveness
in which to move toward everything there is. Nothing
hidden, or hidden from. And, mostly, the days
just glide, like small towns
you drive through, or farms in the Midwest.
Still, there are some things that,
looked back on, rise up, like those hills.
Childhood, a particular spring day after rain.
Mimosa, the trees shaking out their leaves, the faint
sour fruit of earth. Description is the best
you can do, but not enough. It's the feeling
of the day you remember anyway,
the way everything seemed secret and blameless
at once. Just a hint on the clean air
of what you'd have to learn. That something final
had begun, and nothing you would do could make it stop.

# January, 1946

In San Francisco the light comes down the hills
one step at a time, the way a woman walks
slowly home from her last day
at the office, and the light is the color
of her hair. If it weren't cold,
she would take off her shoes, she is that tired.
She puts out her arms to steady herself,
because she is pregnant and because there is something
no one knows. If she could choose, she would be
anonymous as a wave that breaks, for a moment,
against your hand. She would be the stillness
in those clouds massed above the bay.
She thinks she is lucky he never went to sea
while all around her women were left
with children. And now the war is over,
the train feeling its way through tunnels
of fog along the coast, the tracks rusted
with salt, while she lies in her berth
imagining me sleeping inside her, little fish
rocked in the waters under her heart.
Her husband is sleeping too, and how easy
it would be to put on the blue gabardine suit
pinned with a single gardenia turning brown,
now, at the edges, and step off into the yellow dawn
of Los Angeles and disappear. She could get a job
as a secretary somewhere and a little apartment
with a landlady to mind the baby.
She would be no one, a woman nobody knows
who carefully lifts the venetian blind
to look out into the alley, the shadow
already turning the corner. But crossing the desert
she knows what it will be: mowing his parents' yard
every Thursday—every one—and supper afterward.
(The night before I am born
they will argue about it. It will be late May,
already hot, and all she wants is to sit
in her slip in front of the fan and press
ice cubes to her throat, feeling something like a flood
holding her down. She goes, all tears and prickly heat.)
She stares out at the red hills of New Mexico
and thinks they are the same reddish brown
as the blood her mother spit into a handkerchief,
and remembers how her grandfather,

2

told his oldest child had died that night,
whispered only, I know.
When we die, she thinks, the tracks simply stop
somewhere in the middle of a field.
We don't fly up on the backs of white birds
to Heaven, invisible wings brushing
the faces of those we've loved.
Nothing like those white birds
sweeping past the windows of the train.
Waking, she sees it's only snow.
This is winter, and Texas.
Since California, we've traveled a season,
her husband says. We're almost home, she tells him,
and everywhere she looks are frozen fields of wheat
caught, like breath, against the sky.

*for my mother*

# ON FIRE

*Love might ask anything of you*
*Or fire might ask anything of you*
*and say that its name is love.*
                —William Mathews

Someone was *playing with fire,* I'd hear
them whisper and think, amazed, not me.
How much of childhood is spent
trying to learn language
is a metaphor for metaphor, like snow, which is not
itself solely, but the longing
it engenders and endures, and that only
a stand-in for the past. As for fire, I knew
what I feared most: that it turned
to ashes. In winter childhoods you had to be
careful in those houses not built
for cold, gas heaters licking the ice
from the air, someone's white nightgown
tongued red with flame. The winter
my father's old football coach died
in a fire, it was colder.
His friends, ex-players, middle-aged and home
for the funeral, came by to hear my father
tell how the coach pushed his son
out a window to safety just as the roof
collapsed around him, a hero's
unremarkable story. I believed it to be
a given, what any father would do
for his child. In the unheated front room,
usually closed in such weather, the men's tongues
were stiff as bells, as our limbs
before waking. They were men as big
as my father, bigger even, their hands
so huge they could cradle a football
the way they might gently hold a bird,
stunned and sheared with ice, to warm it.
My father wept then, as if
for the first time, not quietly, as when
my small sister lived and died
in an hour, his sobs like stutters in her throat,
but fully, like a man among men.
I'd never seen that grief
before. If I'd known the language

4

I might have said it was playing with fire
to understand just what is given,
what is taken away, but I was
dumb. In the cold room my face burned
as I watched. I was on fire with love
and awe for him and, yes,
with shame.

# RUMORS

In tornado weather, my mother said, the day
goes dark, or half dark, the birds
shut down, and she could see it coming.
She scanned the open palm of the sky
for hours, each cloud a prediction
of bad luck. I saw it coming
even in the dark, those nights the stillness

in the air was the silence of a siren
before the siren sounds. I lay awake
all night to wait it out. How many blasts
for storm, how much for war? I couldn't
get it straight. At school, trained to "duck
and cover," we sat with folded hands
and memorized rules for safety, or drew

poster after paper poster—Crayola flames
and firetrucks, the red, exploding suns
of stoplights—until we won the prize: a visit
from Roy Rogers to "The Nation's Safest School."
In the door of the fourth-grade classroom,
his aging, made-up face rode high
above a fringed white cowboy suit. Once,

in a movie, I saw another man walk out alone
into the street to shoot a dog gone mad
with foam. On the screen that dog looked
almost harmless, a mouth of shaving cream.
Every summer, in rumor, he ran through town, sick
and crazed, closing in on the neighborhood
until my mother kept me in. I watched the street

for dogs all afternoon, the paralyzed shadow
fallen across the scorched grass. Some noons
the siren blew another warning: midday, Mother
believed, polio would catch me out of doors.
Each magazine she read told something else
to shun—heat, crowds, the unwashed body
of the city swimming pool—while I, dumb-struck

by sun, folded to the floor
beneath the Philco's wooden face and waited
for the clock to move. I thought polio

was like that dog, blocks away but coming closer,
or like what my mother called "prowlers"—
not the familiar black-and-white burglars
in cartoons I laughed at in my parents' *Collier's,*

the big, stupid one named Butch bungling everything,
but something else she heard nights
my father was away, shadowed
by the live oak in the corner of the yard.
Almost everyone knew someone lost.
A young mother drifted down the walk, a girl
so beautiful I wanted to be the baby

she carried in her arms. Under the honeysuckle
bush I pinched the cloying blossoms
in my hands. The next week she floated
up to Heaven in a single breath. At dusk
I rode my bicycle to the park and leaned my cheek
against the chain link fence. Drained
for health, the abandoned swimming pool

gaped like the wide mouth
of a movie monster in the almost dark,
its enormous jaws about to swallow
the tiny figures scurrying unsuccessfully
out of reach, just like *The Thing* that sent me
cowering under my seat one Saturday
at the matinee. I imagined a dive, the high board

I'd never dared, the long fall toward water
that wasn't there. Back home, in bed,
I heard the radio crackle the coming storm
and pulled the damp sheet above my head.
I couldn't move. My mother roamed the house,
checking the windows for prowlers, counting
the candles in case the lights went out.

# HOPE

What saves us begins
as something small, the thing
so insignificant we hardly notice.
First letter, a syllable, then another
and another, until what we are rises
through them like a face
a child patiently traces from dot to dot
in a coloring book. It was there
all along, had we but seen it, the way
the constellations are always
in the stars. They shine, cold
and singular, in the late December sky
years after Wittgenstein, in exile,
crosses a bleached field in England
to a cottage where an Irish setter stands
like a copper bust at the moonlit
window. He thinks how the dog knows his master
at the door but not that he will come again
the next day, and the day after that,
into the room that smells of damp fur and wool
where the housekeeper has just laid a fire
in the grate and placed a glass of port
on the table. There must be words for that.
And for this, too, then: for a child who believed
fortunes could be told. The fine web
in the palm, tea's bitter leaves.
What a book called *retromancy*. I had a red coat
and a pocket heavy with keys. When I set out
for school each morning, I stopped
three times and looked over my shoulder
to name it there, I thought, forever:
the gray house surrounded by its grove of ash.
From there, I walked out into the future.
I walked out into the future, though in truth
I was always leaving and coming back,
trying to master memory's thick tongue,
like ancient Greek a difficult language
in which *going* and *coming* are the same word.

# FOURTH OF JULY, TEXAS, 1956

The night was nothing we knew. We'd never seen
such stars, not even there, in Texas.
My mother held the sky maps and leaned
so far back she fell.
She wasn't hurt. Nothing can hurt her,

I thought, who didn't know, and aimed
my flashlight at the night, and shot.
A long way from here to there, years
and years for light to go, my cousin said.
We were little planets

hurled from stars, spinning
and falling. We lay in the grass
and watched the sky revolve
until the words put on their shapes.
High in the western dark, the Teapot tipped
its spout. The Scorpion crept along the floor
so close I lifted up my hand
to brush its tail. And then,

because it was summer and we were children,
we stood on the porch
while the uncles set off fireworks
in the field. My mother sang
their names out: *Clustering Bees,
Southern Blue, Tower of Jewels, Willow Tree.*
She laughed and caught me
in her arms. The sky was somebody's

house, lit from within and bursting, and the stars,
those thousand broken embers, stars
raining down all over us, us and the earth,
what the sky comes down to.

# CHRISTMAS EVE AT ROSEMOUND CEMETERY

And on the graves the poinsettias,
red stars dimming in the cold, as though anything

could cheer the dead. As though they lie
in their beds like children, their faces turned

toward Christmas morning, or wait expectantly,
already dressed for the day

in their flowered prints, in their shiny suits
and slightly frayed collars. You might as well string

colored lights in the bare branches, hang
mistletoe from the headstones, as though a kiss

could wake them, as though they shared
our guilt and loneliness. You might as well

pay them a Christmas visit, or say my grandmother
heard our footsteps on the frozen grass

of Rosemound Cemetery her first year in the ground,
that an old dream of childhood

brought back to her the sound of reindeer
on the roof. That Christmas Eve my mother thought

to bless a new tradition, and so, flushed
with rounds of friends and whiskey, we fell

into the chill air. There was no snow, only
a blank December dusk. There was no one there,

only a family walking off into the future
one member at a time. We didn't touch

or speak. Even my small daughter, let loose
to run, froze in the shadows

of our long faces. I don't know how long
we stood there, or what we thought, if we thought

at all, as the light faltered and no stars
came out, not a single one, and the dead

were beyond our caring. Whatever comfort we hoped
to find there, they wouldn't give it.

You might as well say they drank a toast
to our envy, that they draped their thin arms

across each other's shoulders and laughed
till they cried at how foolish

we were, as though we could ever be
above reproach, like them.

# HOLLOW

I never knew, then, why it was named that,
The Hollow, where the Blacks lived—Coloreds,
we called them—where the road from town crested
the hill and wound down past Miller's Gin for a mile

or so, though it seemed like more, open fields
on either side and beyond the field on the left
the town cemetery, Rosemound Cemetery, past their school
with its broken windows, and then the houses began,

shabby and needing paint, the kind of house
Jeanne Crain might have left to pass for white
in *Pinky* if this were the black-and-white past
of the movies and not Commerce, Texas, in 1955. Even

the poorest had a TV and a Cadillac out front. That's what
we said, anyway, and laughed, making ourselves
blameless, an adult's bland dismissal of a foolish child.
I don't know how they lived, the maids and cooks,

the yardmen, who got their whiskey and fruitcakes,
their ten-dollar bills at Christmas, who had their own
plates and cups and silverware in the houses
where they worked for years. Even their names weren't ours:

Ruby and Opal and Pearl rolling like jewels
off the tongue, or the ludicrous nicknames, Butter
and Sambo—Sambo, who always had a smile and a kind word,
who, proud of his position, dressed in a white coat

to open doors at parties. Their lives were an infinite
mystery to me, the way anything Other is mysterious,
a subject of curiosity, even a little feared. It's all
confused with smells: the musky odor of bodies, the char

of bacon grease and greens, water standing too long
in a ditch, even the clean scent of sprinkled clothes
and starch when Bessie came to iron on Thursdays. I rode
with my mother to take her home, thrilled and scared to be

going there, doors locked and windows shut, and once,
when I started to climb in the backseat, taught
that's where children sat, she almost pushed me down
insisting I get up front with my mother. Today

a woman in a shop where the rich sell their cast-off
clothes for charity told me her cat had disappeared,
stolen, she was sure, by Mexicans. They drive
through the neighborhood, she said, and when they see

a beautiful cat they come back at night and take it.
And I remembered the telephone jokes we played
as children, how we liked especially to call those names
that seemed so funny to us and say something silly—

"Is your refrigerator running? Well, stop it before it gets
away"—and how we once called Bessie at the number
in my mother's book. A neighbor went next door to get her.
I think she must have hurried from her house, surprised

and expectant, her tiny, bird-like legs moving as fast
as seventy years allowed. I don't remember what we said,
but I'm sure we laughed, afterwards, at her confusion,
at the way she talked "like she has a mouthful of marbles."

I didn't know anything, really, about her life, nor
would I, if I could, have willingly entered it, and so
my pity, after all this time, for what she suffered, my shame
for all our ignorance seem somehow like that name, hollow.

# FOUR ROSES

Outside my door four roses
languish in the late spring sun. They don't
smell of failure yet, though he did, who hid
Four Roses in a cardboard suitcase. In memory
they call my uncle "Rabbit" because he runs
like that. Red-faced, he crouches
in the infield, short, and makes the dive
and throws to first. One out. I'm six
and sitting in the bleachers the summer
Eisenhower thought to save the world again, proud
to be his niece. The Fort Worth Cats are all the sport
there is. My father says I have it wrong.
By 1952 the whiskey stopped him, he hadn't played
in years, just coached, and that not much.
But I'd rather believe him home
and safe than think of the day my father,
out with his boss, saw a bum weaving
down a city street, a bottle of Four Roses
in his hand. Something in his walk gave him away.
My father turned back to the road, drove on
and on. The last time I saw my uncle he stooped
and shuffled when he walked, left a pile
of crumbs around his plate. It's an old story.
Next week I'll be forty and he'll be dead
five months who raised Four Roses to his lips
and drank. And what is memory
if not the glare of a sun-drenched field
where an almost Texas Leaguer pops up
and up and Rabbit opens his glove
to catch it, one hand, and end the game?

*(C.W.M. 1910–1985 )*

# Rhythm and Blues

Those days our bodies drove us, churning
the still water of the pond, or long afternoons
wading a hill blue with berries. We lay
in the sun assessing every word
or look, pretending not to see the way
wind lifted fine blond hairs on a leg, how
a muscle rippled beneath the flesh. Water to land
and back again, we could never be cool

enough. Shy and sweet-faced, what was it
we wanted? Not to be like that. We couldn't wait
for night to fall. Supper over, the slow talk
winding down, we fled the family's satisfied table
to cruise those country roads in twos or fours
or tens, whatever kept us not alone. We were cool
then, stolen whiskey and cigarettes and the radio's
red glow, we were trouble

waiting to happen. Music those nights was anything
black and staticky and far away and blind
Ray Charles had seen the light.
We'd never stop loving her, or him, and love
was only misery, but we pretended not to care.
We shouted "Hit the Road, Jack!" and floorboarded
the Chevy Carry-all around another curve, wise
in our ignorance. It wouldn't have helped to know

how many times we'd really have to sing the blues
in twenty years, that the object changes
but desire persists. That some of us
would die too soon. It wouldn't have helped to know
tonight the sun would still be
going down like teenagers in the backseat
of a father's borrowed Chevy, burning,
every part of them on fire.

# EGGS

Morning broke like an egg
on the kitchen floor and I hated
    them, too, eggs, how easily they broke
and ran, yellow insides spilling out, oozing

    and staining, the flawed
beneath what's beautiful. And I hated
    my father, the one cock
in the henhouse, who laid the plate

    on the table and made me
eat, who told me not to get up
    until I was done, every bite. And I hated
how I gagged and cried, day

    after day, until there was no time
left and he'd give in and I'd go off
    to school like that, again, hungry.
But why did I hate eggs

    so much? Freud, old banty rooster, who knew
a thing or two about such things, might say
    I hated myself, hated the egg
growing in secret deep inside my body,

    the secret about to be spilled
to the world, and maybe I did.
    Or maybe it's the way the egg
repeats itself again and again, a perfect

    oval every time, the way I imagined myself,
furious, standing by my own child's bed
    holding a belt, and saw her face
dissolve in a yolk. But that doesn't say

    enough about why we hoard
our hurts like golden eggs and foolishly
    wait for them to hatch, why
we faced each other across the table,

    my father and I, and fought
our battles over eggs and never fought
    with them, never once picked up
those perfect ovals and sent them singing

back and forth across the room, the spell
broken like shells, until we were
    covered with them, our faces golden
and laughing, both of us beautiful and flawed.


*for Stephen Dunn*

# ONLY CHILDHOOD

It was only childhood, I could say and mean
by that two things at once, its insignificance
and singularity. But we all know it wasn't
insignificant: how else explain the habits
we've become? And still we're named
by our place at the table. Oldest
of six, youngest of three, the middle child.
An only child. It's singular because it's yours
alone and singular if you're all alone,
though we're all lonely and so not
singular. I started to say there's no loneliness
like a child's, but there is.
Mostly, you still believe someone
will come and, mostly, they do.
Even from love, they come.
Under the door, the lights go out
and the muffled sounds, a growl
in the throat, and the radio goes up, somebody's
saxophone weeping "Body and Soul," and a cry
rises on one long note. Then the lights
go on in the upstairs hall and my mother
passes my door, open now, holding her nightgown
bunched at her hips.

And what did it have to do
with me, their only child? Through the blinds
bars of light laid down a ladder
on my floor. I could climb it right
to sleep if I wanted. Maybe I'd find the place
God keeps our souls when we're asleep, though
I was afraid of being taken there and never
coming back. *If I should die*
*before I wake* . . . . But how could God take
what was already His to keep?
I closed my eyes and tried to imagine
what the soul was, and where, the something
that makes you you, my father said.
The world and I seemed so much
the same I didn't understand and yet
I thought it must be true. I thought
my father was the world. When the dark
reached out its tentacles around my bed, he came
and held me in his arms and there was nothing

left to fear. I climbed the ladder
into sleep. The opposite of *soul* was *body*,
a place I touched and then was punished for.
This went on, I think, for years and the world
outside seemed very far away.

       It was only childhood.
In the photograph album, there, in full sunlight,
my father holding me up looks like
he's holding . . . something. When did I learn
to distrust the world, its love
and shame? I wasn't even looking.

*for Cynthia Macdonald*

# NEW HOPE

They called it New Hope, who hadn't much,
save the windswept hill
where they buried their dead, my mother's
mother's family. They believed they'd rise up
come Judgment Day, and this was as good a place
as any, a head start they might have thought,
looking out across the scorched pastures
over all Dallas County, what their patriarch called
The Promised Land. Above the graves, the insufficient
shade: straggling pecans, scrub oak, a mesquite
or two, the stubborn tree which gave the nearby town
its name. Like pioneers, it won't give up, roots
thrusting down through fifty feet of rocky soil
to quench their thirst. And maybe to him
it did seem a kind of Eden just because
he'd settled there and done all right, this boy
who lit out from Kentucky and took for himself
the local gentry's name, as though the word
and thing were one. I imagine him dressing for the trip
in a clean white shirt, his one good suit, shiny
and threadbare, folded neatly in his satchel,
how such things would matter. He will never look
back to where his father leans on the fence, spits
a fat stream of juice in the dust
stirred by the horses' hooves, shrugs and turns
away. It was, really, the most interesting thing
about him, the little detail of character, the flaw,
that brings the narrative to life. Otherwise,
his tale was dull as the lives of good men
always are: he loved his wife and raised
ten children, outlived four, owned a cotton gin
and prospered some, though much of his money
he gave away. At 95, he died, "a saint,"
his children said, speaking of him
in hushed tones reserved for the irreproachable dead
those Sunday afternoons they tended the family plot.
I was bored, itchy with heat. Wandering
among the plain, unassuming stones, I wanted stories,
not facts, dates of birth and death, but something
I didn't have a name for then. Where was
the mystery, the life gone wrong? Here, they said,
the black sheep converted on the battlefields of France,
a Protestant boy from Texas who roamed

among the heaped dead making the sign of the cross,
his hand raised shyly in the unfamiliar gesture,
until he took a bullet in the heart. Or here, a girl
buried in her wedding gown, left at the church
by a young man who'd come back in twenty years—rich
then, with horses stamping at the gate—to beg forgiveness,
not knowing she drowned herself the day he left.
Now those stories seem too neat, like graves
swept clean and lined with tinfoil-potted plants,
told to satisfy a child years before the city
swallowed up the hill, cheap apartment houses
staggering along the road, gas stations and bowling alleys,
bars and "Adult Books Open All Night" and everyone you see
looks like people on the news, the ones
shoved into police cars just after pictures
of the child's back tattooed by cigarettes.
A mile away in her apartment my aunt was robbed
and left for dead, her face hammered out like a piece of tin.
Today my father wept into the phone.
My mother dead ten months, he's remembering how
six years ago last week she sobered up.
He can't forget, he says.
Why should he? In another cemetery
he bends to tend her grave, rakes up
the leaves and puts a pot of zinnias out.
The hot October wind blows everything away.

## SUNDAY NIGHTS

The man I married grew sad
every Sunday night. Even in summer a cloud
enveloped him. Something about his past,
he said, something about his childhood.
It always is. It's so American, that loneliness,
that longing. Friday the weekend stretches
before us like a new world, green

with its promise: the family together, maybe
neighbors in for a drink, a little peace. By Sunday
we're at land's end—storms, wars, a pestilence
of words. Nothing is what we imagined.
I remember childhood Sunday nights,
the long church day over, how good it felt
to be warm inside a house

the color of a pigeon's breast, or nodding
over Sunday supper, chipped beef on toast or tamales
bought from the town's one Mexican
Saturdays on the square, and my father asleep
in the TV's dull green gaze, my mother
complaining of divas who sang in foreign tongues.
A ritual predictable as every day was then:

Lassie, Jack Benny, Ed Sullivan and off to bed.
Today's the last Sunday in September and everything
is falling, the temperature, the rain. All day
it's been coming down, this change
of seasons, though I see by the weather map
it hasn't reached you yet, a thousand miles away.
The last night we were together

it was Sunday and I came late to your door
like a bad movie. (This is the part where the train
pulls out of the station in a cold rain and someone
is betrayed, or someone's lost, and all
the handkerchiefs come out.) Nothing is what
we imagined. Neither of us was wrong,
or wronged, and there's nothing to be said

about it, and everything, as someone said of death.
Don't get me wrong, I know it's not the same,
that Sunday is just the night before Monday.

Still, I can't help thinking how that movie might end:
the train is stopped just in time by a telegram,
its message clear as the forecast. It's the one
where someone's sorry and asks to be forgiven:

*Come back*, it hums, *come back, my continent,
my love, my heart's desire, you know
I'm all you've ever wanted.*

# Too Good to Be True

Small towns in Texas have names
too good to be true. On Sunday drives
we'd pass the signs for Bug Tussle
and Jot 'Em Down but never see the towns.
Scattered houses, maybe a grocery
with an empty pump, one church—
certain to be Baptist—they became
their names, common and temporary.
No doubt someone has traced
their origins and put them
in a book, but I don't want to know.
I'd rather imagine a farmer
looking out at cotton fields flattened
by hail or torched by sun, who thinks
to himself they aren't worth enough
for boll weevils to fight over. Or,
a man writes down the possible names
of towns but can't come to a decision,
though one he discards is Emblem, chosen
by a girl who picks a sprig of crape myrtle
to remind her what happened in the garden
among the shrubs and laden trees.

Some things seem so right
they're wrong, telling us so much
about themselves there's nothing left
to be said about them, or believed.
That sign hung for years above the courthouse:
"The Blackest Land, The Whitest People."
Black was for soil, the rich earth that would grow
anything, and white meant only
a kind of neighborliness. If someone did a favor,
you might respond, "That's white of you."
Anyway, that was the explanation.
"Even our niggers are white," they said,
in Greenville. So fact becomes stranger
to fiction and can't survive our imagination
of it. That's why stories are told
in families, but never written down, leaving
no room for doubt, like a young man
who walks into a general store
one summer day in, maybe, nineteen-ought-two,
as they used to say. He's a farmer,

and poor, because the storms and heat
have ruined his cotton. But he's happy,

you can see it in his face, and he's about
to be married. He wears a sprig
of crape myrtle in his lapel, and he enjoys
so much telling a story about his grandfather,
who went to California in '49 and came back
rich. The bridles were sterling silver,
he says, the plates were gold. *And then,*
so every story goes, *and then,*
the grandfather went to war and took
his slave and never came back from that.
An old black man leaning on the counter
begins to weep, tears filling the ditches
of his face, "I am the slave," he says,
"who went with your grandaddy to the war."
No one believes him. Not a young man
who wears his happiness like luck,
or a wedding, nor the farmers talking idly
through the long afternoon about failure
and the weather, who shrug and look
away, trying to forget, for just a moment,
that things that once seemed right
can turn out wrong, or how a life might prove
to be a long and rambling story, too true
any longer to be good.

# KNOWING THE END

It's like knowing a girl named Roxy,
you said, to hear the plot before you see
the movie. Say a man is sitting in a bar in Cleveland
late some night and he's lost count
how many shots of Black Jack
he's knocked back and he's too many sheets
to the wind to care. The Indians, picked
to win the East, are locked up
in the cellar once again. They've thrown away
the key. The bartender asks him if he wants
another and he says, Sure, why not, after all
he's Chief of the Bureau of Lost Causes.
Then down the bar he sees her, eyes
green as the underside of a new leaf, a mini-skirt
hiked up to show six inches of white thigh
creamy as a wedding cake. He likes the way
her red hair swings against her back
when she bends to light a Kool, then cocks it
in the air and sips some fancy drink, maybe
a sloe gin fizz. He sidles over and offers
to buy her a refill. She's seen a few like him
too many, but she'd like to have some fun.
He's already a goner. She's a secretary
who wanted to be an actress, but what the hell,
L.A.'s too far away and, besides, she's heard
those stories of the casting couch. She's saving
for Club Med. Her name's Roxy, she says, and right away
he sees the future: maybe a few nights
in an apartment with two cats and lady's lingerie
sprouting like Queen Anne's lace on the bathroom's
snowy field and before long she's working overtime
and coming home at 2 A.M. Someone calls
and when he answers, they hang up. Pretty soon
he's sitting on this stool again and he's lost
count how many shots of Black Jack he's knocked back.
He knew it all the time, he tells the bartender.
Isn't he the Chief? Hey, he wrote the script.
Let's face it, friend, it wouldn't take a girl
like that to break his heart. Anything could
do it. Still, wasn't it sweet those nights they lay
entangled on her flowered sheets and wasn't he brave
to believe it? It's the hope we have
to live with, why we keep on waking up

to think today neither the Indians nor love
will disappoint, though now we know every plot
by heart and still, before we're ready
the climax comes, the screen goes dark.

*for Lee Abbott*

# PINETUM

All afternoon I've walked these fields
of Christmas trees trying to recall the exact
shape of happiness. I'm remembering
my father reaching out to set in place
the treetop star, a paper one, gold,
that followed us year to year, a childhood's

length of days, until it disappeared. The time
my mother bought an artificial tree, flocked
with fake-snow paint and hung with satin apples,
I said it wasn't Christmas. So children make
of rituals a way to give anticipation
form, and more, it stayed our fears, so much

beyond our small powers to reason:
we would always rise in the dark
to a cold house and an empty plate and find
the tree waiting to be lit, the gifts laid out
before us. We know it now as falling in love,
though we wonder why we call it *falling,*

the brief time it takes to think perfection
possible and love a way to manage
fear. We believe then we will always rise
to the body, the heart held out
in the palm, as what you love includes
these trees, even the smallest one that stands

off to itself a little, and doesn't need you.
Now the sun climbs down its ladder of sky
cloud by cloud and hovers over the pine's spire
like a gold star someone set in place.
The light in the room grows dim.
Your son lingers at supper, dreaming

of the groundhog he watched you trap
today among rows of seedlings. Leaning
against your arm, he asks, *Do parents ever
die before their boys grow up?*
We shake our heads, looking away
to the window. Night now, and winter's

first snow is just coming down, a little
drift through the branches. We can't see it

in the dark. We know by now how small
our powers are, though we're still afraid
of what we won't name, still
saved by the white, irresistible lies.

*for Marshall and Cindy Stacey*

# MATINEE

There's that moment in *To Catch a Thief*
when Grace Kelly surprises Cary Grant
with a kiss and we know she's in control.
She's an heiress, he's a jewel thief, but for all
her cold, imperial blondness, the sexual
belongs to her. She tells him he might see
one of the Riviera's greatest sights and she's
right, the heat in those blue eyes,
the way she drapes the long chiffon
scarf across a bosom more ample than a girl
from Main Line Philadelphia has any right to.
He never had a prayer. In 1955
she's still a year away from being
Princess Grace, a wedding my grade-school class
will watch on television, a story also
more American than we could know. The first time
I saw that movie I didn't understand,
nor why the blond-haired girl who'd never been
my friend asked me to see it after school, nor why
her father joined us there. Weren't all fathers
working weekday afternoons? In the darkened theater
he sat between us, an ordinary, gray-haired man,
his khaki work clothes streaked with oil
and grease, the rank, male sweat
of the gas station. Maybe it was that exact
moment when Grace Kelly kissed Cary Grant
he took my hand and held it
to his lap and I felt something
burrowing there, slick and blind, like the kittens
black Trouble gave birth to in a box
in our garage. I didn't move or say a word
but stared straight ahead and let him
hold me there until the final credits rolled, the way
for years afterward I stared unseeing at the world's
blank screen and let life press against me and took
whatever came. Outside the Palace Theater dusk
had fallen, night spread like a stain
across the red brick streets of my hometown, a world
grown suddenly dark and strange.

# PIRATE'S BEACH

If Lafitte did bury treasure on this beach
maybe it still shines deep under the dark sand, the way
clusters of foam left by the tide this morning
made prisms in the sun. Taking on the colors
of the day—the blue of ocean, pinkish-brown of sand—
they seem wholly imagined, the surprise and polish
of memory embellished to become a story we tell.
And it's the particulars that give the story
weight. Not the idea of gold coins
to be found years later by a beachcomber
down on his luck, or of a pirate who died
before he could reclaim his lost reserve,
but complications of the plot. Say he had a woman
waiting in Galveston, black eyes watching
the door, but she's disappeared from history,
that Mexican whore, and his is legendary, bespeaking
a lack of character. So we must invent them
night after night in some back room trying so fiercely
to obliterate the body, those for whom flesh
is a kind of judgment. When she closes her eyes,
she thinks of a handsome young priest

whose scent was rosewater placing the wafer gently
on her tongue. Or sees the cold stars suspended
above her village, the hills exploding
with gunfire, the burning cedar and piñon. He wakes
before dawn and remembers a peasant he saw as a boy
stomped to death by a horse. He had no face, no mouth
with which to scream, and still his cries filled
the air, until the boy raised his hands to his ears
and screamed and screamed in answer, as if to drown
out sound. Now he only wants to be alone,
so he moves against her the way the waves thrust
against the shore in last night's storm, impersonally,
to wear it down. Walking on the beach
this morning, lost in that story awhile, I remembered
a man I'd loved and how he talked
about his childhood, its shame and pain. How
his father's drinking hurt him, what it was like
to be afraid. Holding him then, I loved most
his sadness, a secret life words can't say.
And isn't that what we love in another, that ache
that can't be filled, because, after all, it's what
we love in ourselves? If memory is belief,

then the stories we tell about our lives may finally
become true, the ones where we think we'll die of love,
and wake like sleepwalkers, surprised in our bodies,
opening our eyes, suddenly, alone, in the dark.

# PROVINCETOWN

Off Provincetown, in June, the whales
swim right up to the boat. Music
excites them or the exclamations
of tourists. Whatever
does it, they fall and rise again
and again, without sound, coloring
the sea just before they surface
the brilliant aquamarine seen only
in paintings. Delicately, they arc
their great bulks through the water, waving
their tails like hands. We imagine it
as a greeting, and wave back.
How graceful they are, the way
a fat man who's a good dancer is graceful,
defying the laws of gravity. Though
there are two of them and we like to think
of them as mates, we don't know
their histories, the seasons they've come
to this calm place, but that first time
together, I could believe everything:
that we would return summer
after summer and find those same two
whales making a kind of blessing
with their bodies, or that love would be
enough to buoy us in this life.
As we were buoyed when, later,
we watched a small flotilla of fishing boats
dressed in their feast-day clothes, their red
and blue and yellow coats striping
a thin rainbow on the water. On each
of them, the Portuguese fishermen stood
in their new white shirts, their violent faces
in repose. Above them, the priest made
the sign of the cross, that they might go
another year into the cold, rough waters
to gather in again the black nets
heavy with food, that their sons
and their sons' sons might return without harm
to be many times blessed. I thought then
how faith forms in the body before it rises
to our lips as words, or prayer.
And always, the form of ceremony, body given
and body taken back. This is for a pledge

made in a week, what they call in your country
*a finger-cutting promise,* sealed flesh
to flesh and bone to bone. And for
its punishment, the thousand needles
that the false must swallow whole.
The true subject of our lives
is time, how little there is of it. And
of the poem too, for it too is
a kind of life. Anything that stops the long
drift of the body, even for a moment, that thing
shall be blessed. Whales in the salt spray,
black ink on a white field, a rainbow
arc of boats. Our hands that bear another.
May our words be air out of water, silver
needles blown on the sea wind.
As each time we come together,
we might remember a man
coughing blood in our hotel in Provincetown,
how the room filled
with the odor of his death, and how,
after they took him away, we lay
on our bed in the tattered light and let
the sea-dank breeze lift over us,
each shared breath repeating
the only litany it knew: If life is a body,
this is its heart we hold in our four hands.

# READING *DAVID COPPERFIELD*

*Whether I shall turn out to be the hero of my own life, or whether that station*
*will be held by anybody else, these pages must show.*

Tonight David is imprisoned
in his room, the fifth night he's been
locked up like that, hearing the rain falling
in the churchyard like grimy tears
that will splatter on his bread and butter
the morning he's sent away to school.
Your son holds my hand and listens
to you read, one chapter in an education
at a time. He can't believe anyone
could be that mean. He'd have bitten
Mr. Murdstone too, he says.

I want to tell him that
I know how the story ends, everything
turns out fine, the boy a man and famous
writer, a husband and a father, but even parents
can't make promises and I'm no parent here, only
his father's visiting lover. He asks where I'm sleeping,
about to offer to share his bed. You tell him
his friends sleep with him and yours with you.
He almost fathoms his unschooled heart.

He wants to father and mother
everything. Last spring, when the male hamster
chewed his cage and scratched the female's eye,
he wept in breath-stopping gulps, not because
she was hurt, he told you, but because
he wanted an eye for an eye and hated himself
for that. It's hard to be a just god, ruling
a universe of hamsters and gerbils, of rockets
and spacemen circling his room all night.

Chapter over, he stumbles
to his closet, time for one last look
at his children. We're not gods, we're not
prepared for what he finds: one gerbil dead,
the other eating it. The topics of today's lesson:
Sex and Death. It's a wonder we don't all fail
growing up. He's inconsolable, sobs
he never wants another thing

to love. How can we tell him that he will,
that memory fades like cane marks
on a boy's back, nights he wept alone
in his room? This isn't a story
to be read before a good-night kiss, someone
turning out the light, closing the door.

He cries himself to sleep.
Later, you turn to me and I wonder if we'll hurt
each other. An educated guess says yes.
And what's the next question? If we could read
the future, I believe that we would be
those gods and not human, as we are, trying
so hard to get it right, the way a boy
puzzles all day over his tear-streaked slate,
marking it, rubbing it out.

# Nineteen

Nothing matters, he says, nothing
anybody does matters, that's why it makes no sense
to try to change things. Maybe he's right,
I think, but we have to hope, don't we, how could we
bear it otherwise? It's so hard to be
nineteen, I haven't forgotten
the powerlessness, all that sexual
longing that makes you feel as if you're burning
from the inside out. Nineteen, a child
really, I fought all year with a boy,
whether to love him or not. Reader, I married him.
This boy reads Nietzsche—I don't
have to ask, I know it—and can't separate
personal freedom, responsibility, from the good
of the state. Who can? I, for instance,
his teacher, would like, right now, to touch
the fine down on his bare thigh just beneath
his khaki shorts, the brown legs too long
for the chair. In China, I tell the class, one child
per family. It's a good rule, he says, or else
we will procreate ourselves clear
out of existence. What are the rights
of the individual, I ask? What would Hitler say?
He says he's tired, there's a point
when he just can't think about these things
anymore, it seems so useless, and I can't think
about them anymore, either, the twenty-plus years
that separate us, my own desire and the claims
of others. We've all known ones like this, so far
down in the excavation of the self they can't dig
free, but this boy doesn't seem the type:
usually they're skinny or too fat, pasty maybe,
a face bubbling with acne, but this one's
beautiful—tall and strong-limbed, though awkward
still (that's part of his charm), the huge, dark eyes
and enviable lashes, full lips. He doesn't know
how much we'll want him. There's something wrong
at the heart of things, he says. He's reading Derrida,
who calls the world *logocentric,* and this is spoken
with a kind of awe, the hush of nothing
left to say. I don't ask him what
he means, if he knows. I've never understood
Derrida exactly, and maybe I can't, but I know

the grammar of desire, how the heart longs
to fill and be filled, and the body,
the way I want this moment to take him in my arms
like a mother, I want to take him in my arms
like a lover, I want to show him
how much love matters, subject and object,
and the fine down on a bare thigh.

# BIRTHRIGHT

At 2 A.M. the train begins its whistle somewhere
outside a small Canadian town and a boy
who might grow up to be you wakes from a dream
about his father. He doesn't want to think of that.
Instead he thinks of the men inside those boxcars
going to Toronto, or maybe Montreal, imagines
himself in Montreal and a beautiful Quebecoise
walking two white dogs by the cathedral.
Suddenly a car, a black Packard, speeds crazily
around the corner, veers onto the sidewalk,
and a second after he pulls her to safety
comes to rest in the very spot where she's been standing.
Perhaps she'll take him home and raise him
as her own. Where did his father go?
Maybe he left Vancouver and the sea behind him and took
the same train to Montreal. Or maybe he sailed
his ship to California, where the boy was born
but which he doesn't remember. It's a secret
he hasn't told anyone yet, the way a detective
in a story gathers a mystery's clues close

to his chest like a hand of cards. He hears the train
whistle once again and thinks of the colored map
above the teacher's desk, the wide spaces between
towns out west. He can't remember much,
except his mother crying. He was a good boy,
she said. Down the hall his uncle turns
in his sleep and snores. Or farts.
The boy can still smell the leftover pot roast
and boiled potatoes. The heavy, overcooked food.
It is so cold in the room he can see
his breath in the moonlight. The cold stings
his cheek, or maybe it is stinging
where his uncle slapped him for making things up,
reading those no-good books that put ideas
in his head. Someday he will have all the books
he wants. The train whistles once more,
and is gone. This is invention, what can be made
from what is known, though all of this
is true, the way a dime in Georgian Bay, Ontario,
would buy Saturday afternoons in worlds

more real than this one. Pearl White outwits
the leering villain once again and Chaplin turns

his sad face so slowly the boy holds
his breath and feels Chaplin's tears thicken
his lashes. Movies are made in California,
where that boy was born, remember, and where
one day he might return. He'll discover soon enough
how we take the past with us wherever we go,
like a hobo who ties up in a bandanna
what's left of a lifetime's belongings
so that he can carry them inside his coat
next to his heart, while he rides trains all over
North America, lonely, looking for something he's lost.
Say a man wants to visit a place he can't
recall. He falls asleep on a train and wakes
to see Santa Barbara spread open beneath him
like some exotic woman. Or he thinks
of a woman's thighs and watches the sun
lie down in the Pacific, stretching itself
slowly across the purple hills and lush green

lawns, the red glut of bougainvillea
and oleander, yellow mustard springing up
between the rocks. Such riotous beauty.
Someone is always lost.
Mother murders every wish and we never
need feel guilt for wanting Father dead
or someone else. Why he won't come home
is clear. The detective, that mild, sad man,
always tells the truth and anything could happen.
After all, this is the same Pacific
where bodies wash up on the beach at night
like so much flotsam, or where a sea captain
takes his son on a boat one summer morning
in Vancouver. It is 1919, and the boy
is so small he can't reach the boat's wheel
or look out at a world turned sky and ocean.
He wants so much to steer, to surge
through the blue water. His father lifts him
onto a chair and places the childish hands
on the wheel. Then he covers them with his own.

*Kenneth Millar (Ross Macdonald) 1915–1983*

# CAMPO SANTO

This far south November
might just as well be summer
some days, it's that green
and hot. Leaves don't turn
here, or fall, drifting down to be raked
into bonfires of their own color.
Weeks from now we'll look up
and—suddenly, it seems—find them
gone, we won't know where.
That's what I thought of, seeing you,
your son two months dead. How,
from now on, you'll look up
from whatever you're doing—planting
bulbs of pale narcissus, say, or
scattering food for the family of ducks
that floated down river to live
in the reeds behind your house—and find
yourself, surprised again, flush
against his absence.

A day like any other. Today, for instance,
sweating, we bent and stooped like gardeners,
papering his grave with flowers,
blue for iris, yellow for daisy, even
the white lily so beautiful
we plant it in the hands of the dead.
You wanted, you said, to see it from the road.

Across town, in the Mexican cemetery,
every grave is piled high like this
with paper flowers, so gaudy
and touching the hills bloom
all year long. It is not because they are poor,
you see, but because they love the dead
that much. It seems, from the road, really
to be a garden. *Campo santo,* they call it,
*holy field,* and even those without belief
say it is blessed by the dead who lie there,
because, surely, all of them were loved once
by someone. Some of them are still remembered.

The Mexican boys who were your son's friends
come each night to this field.

They bring offerings, cigarettes and beer, play
their loud music for him to hear. They leave
letters pressed under stones.
To them, it is holy, dying young
in this man's world. It was just beginning
for them, this world, the day they stood
in a crowd of mourners, their faces stunned
and open above the starched white shirts.
For us, it had continued.

When I drove away from your house that day
I heard the Bach concerto for two violins,
the first violin low and then another,
higher, piercing, and then both of them
together, answering what will not be
consoled. I stopped the car and wept
because I could do nothing else.
There were months we had been like strangers
to each other, distant and awkward, though
I could not say why. Now it had ended,
and I remembered a story a friend had told me,
how when he was young he had loved
a Beethoven sonata so much he had played it
every day, again and again. And then, somehow,
he didn't play it anymore—went away, maybe,
or lost the record, and in time forgot.
Driving across the Bay Bridge ten years later,
he heard it suddenly, after all
those years, on the radio and was overcome
by grief for all that he had lost.

I thought of that again this evening
when we went down to the river.
It was not yet dark, the air
gray and slick with the coming chill.
You stood on the bank and held out
your hand. I stood away from you a little,
watching, because the ducks will not come
for anyone but you. The large brown one,
the male, came to you and gravely
began to eat from your hand, as though
being careful not to hurt you.
I saw then that nothing could

comfort you. Not your friends
who love you, not this life
you will go on living.
I don't know how else to say this.
Which is the greater sorrow, to feel
you can't live without him or to find,
after all, that you can?

# CIVILIZATION

1.

The mother kneels and bends
to her task, tying
the boy's red tennis shoes as if
to root him to the ground,
to her. On the grass he stretches
away from her, naked
except for his shoes and brown socks.
His head is turned away, he doesn't
see her. She is nothing
to him. Already he feels
his power, that body
so different from hers, those hands
which one day could snap her neck
like a bird's. He will not be small
and vulnerable for long. She is
giving him his escape. When she is
done, he will run away
in his red tennis shoes. See,
already he is leaving her.

2.

The mother focuses on the boy and presses
the shutter. "Smile!" she says.
He pulls down his eyes, sticks out his tongue.
She'd told him if he made a face his face
would freeze like that, would turn
to stone and he would be
ugly, ugly, her beautiful boy,
the whites of his eyes blind
to the world. She'd told him
if he stuck out his tongue a bird
would come—a big, black one
with a yellow beak like a knife—
and cut it off. In the civilizing stories
of childhood Mother is always
right and the bad boy gets
what he deserves. He cries wolf
too many times and the wolf's
yellow jaws loom above him, suddenly,
like the cold and terrifying moon. He thinks
it is only a story. She'd told him

if he touched himself, there, in secret,
he would also go blind. He can still see.
So he turns that face to her,
to the world, as if to prove once more
she is lying, Mother is always lying.

# IMMERSION

In the stained glass window behind the choir loft
John baptized Jesus in the river.
The preacher's eyes were blue as Jesus's,
and being immersed meant dying
and being reborn. I could imagine death
that Easter, cold and lank as the water
in the baptistery or white as the handkerchief
he held to my mouth before
he pushed me under. I thought we shared
a secret, and Saturday afternoons lost at the movies,
when the hero returned to find that someone,
Indians or Pancho Villa's men, had burned him
to the ground and his wife and children disappeared,
I tried to understand it. Later, it was no secret,
the old story everybody knew: how the preacher fell
in love and had to leave the church, though
he didn't leave his wife, but took her,
bitter and resigned, and drifted
south to the camps of migrant workers,
where he dispensed the gospel and did
what healing he could, and where, outside a cantina,
I imagine two men are fighting over a woman.
The preacher shoves his way through the crowd
to a man lying on the ground.
He thinks if he could look
into the hole where the man's throat was
he could see the sky, he would see
God, but there is blood
everywhere. Here is a man dying.
He wants to stop the wound but his hand
slips inside it to the knuckle, and above him
is the moon, red and round as the head
of John the Baptist on the plate
and the great clouds scudding across it
are Salome whirling and whirling and the message
is always the same: for love
you must pay with your life.

# LATE-BLOOMERS

It doesn't know it's time
for everything to die, this Rose of Sharon.
Late afternoon September, pink and blooming, it hugs
the sun side of the house. Whatever it is—
a weed, a tree, what the almanac calls a shrub—
it's like a woman in love, bony and too tall,
a little horse-faced even, who's accustomed to knowing
she isn't beautiful. She's surprised by this
sudden flowering, the last one before the frost.
I know what it is to be
a wallflower, a weed, the one girl nobody

danced with Friday nights. At twelve
my friend had breasts and a bad case
of cramps. On the sixth grade trip to Fair Park Zoo
Roy Presley kissed her in the darkened bus
so long I shut my eyes and prayed
I'd be changed like that.
This morning, in the library's cool vault, I held
in my hands another prayer, the book
Anne of Cleves gave Henry when, impatient

for his bride, he waylaid her
on the road to London, surprising her, he said,
"to nourish love," as if to test the truth
of Holbein's portrait—a gaze at once so frank
and so demure it seemed to promise mysteries
even a king had never guessed. On the flyleaf,
in tiny, birdlike scrawl, she'd written,
*I beseech your most humble grace,*
*whenever you look on this, remember me,*
but what he remembered was his anger,
disappointment that she was not beautiful

as the artist saw her, the golden sun surpassing
Christine of Denmark's silver moon, but a woman
no longer young, "a Flanders mare."
When he gave her 4,000 pounds and freedom
not to please, she began to grow into the painting.
Holbein hadn't dreamed her
after all, had only seen something sleeping
in those hooded eyes. Oh, I know some things
don't change. At our twentieth class reunion

the same girl is still the one they judge
Most Beautiful, the one to whom the football boys,
those who came back from Vietnam, incline
their balding heads and paunching bellies. "Beauty is
in the eye of the beholder," my mother said,
but I begin to believe it's in the one
beheld, the way love, however late, shows us
our truest selves, the way the blossom sleeps
inside the bud. This poem, then, is for her
who doesn't think she's beautiful enough, for Anne,
for me, this weedy shrub, for all late-bloomers.

# DISTANCES

Now time has made us,
if not friends, at least not enemies,
I wake in our old house while you're away
and go downstairs for coffee and the *Post,*
the children I've come to stay with still asleep.
In the early light the room assumes
its familiar shape, and I open every window
and door closed against last night's storm
to the rain-soaked, steamy world. Each piece
of furniture stays where it was, even this sofa
I slept on nights before I left.
Afterwards, I dreamed for years
of coming back. Nothing had changed, though
in the dream's blue film our room seemed
to have lost its sharp edges. You were beside me
under the green spread I never liked, and everything
floated like objects seen underwater. This isn't
what I wanted, I'd think and try to struggle
up from sleep's black undertow until, awake,
I'd be flooded by relief. Alone
in another city, I wandered through rooms
of a furnished sublet, dazed with gratitude
and disbelief, touching things as though
the unfamiliar shapes could give to me myself:
two ducks, lamps lit from within, waddled
across the floor and a wooden circus train
never stopped traveling, each tiny animal
safe and perfect in its separate cage.
The walls smelled like trees. Sometimes
I remember another dream, the old dream
of falling: at six, told Freddie Harbour's brother
slipped from the library's third-floor rail, I fell
night after night, the marble floor reaching up for me.
In that dream I never hit bottom, never tested
the warning that to dream of the end
of falling is to die in your sleep. I don't believe
it's true. I'm here and still alive.
         ∿

We used to say this house
had ghosts. Signs so common they might be a story
by someone without imagination: footsteps
on the stairs, a door creaking and closing

by itself, a visitor we sometimes sensed in sleep.
But if ghosts are the imagined shadows
of ourselves, then maybe I was the ghost, disembodied
and beside myself, drifting through days
like drifting through walls. Even now, I'd say
our spirits hover here, linger
over things we carried house to house and city
to city—a hand-carved chair, the Picasso print
we loved, a box of photographs, though
there is no photograph now of your face
as a shut gate, your body as a wall
I couldn't climb. Maybe our lives,
as they always have, accumulate in small things.
The angle, for instance, with which the sun flares
this morning through the east windows, each mote
moving and separate in the light.
Months after our last move we found
our album of wedding pictures had vanished
as though it never was, and I imagine it
taken up by a drunk in an abandoned warehouse.
He nurses his bottle and carefully turns
the pages. How happy they look, he thinks, sentimental
as a drunk can be. How beautiful everyone is!
The bridesmaids smiling above their pink dresses, the
groomsmen who laugh and hold themselves
toward the camera with a deliberate grace
he recognizes. Can he tell, in that picture, you're blushing
because with each handshake they press condoms
into your palm like money? Perhaps he does
or does not notice that I have the stunned,
unfocused look I wore so often then, or that,
in this picture, I'm putting your ring on the wrong hand.
            ᨑ

Once a friend told me
how a man she loved lived on for years
in the house his wife and children left and how
on her bedroom wall one of his daughters
had drawn with black crayon the outline of a heart
and inside a kind of epitaph:
*A whole family once lived here,* with all their names
and the date. When she saw it, she said,
she knew what it meant to have a past

you can never forgive. There's nothing like that
here, only the old records I left behind. I wipe away
the dust and put the Stones on the stereo.
"You can't always get what you want,"
they wail. Mick puckers his lips
and struts. We didn't believe them then,
those old songs of frustration, and it still
sounds like a joke, the way he teases
the words, though the joke's, I guess, on us.
That summer Brian Jones drowned at Cotchford Farm
was the hottest I remember, though I've forgotten
plenty. I was pregnant and numb, weighted down
by a life that wasn't mine. All summer I read
*Winnie-the-Pooh,* a kind of mourning, in preparation.
I wanted, like him, to know it "by heart,"
as we say. We mean by that to commit it
to memory, as if desire alone could tell us
what we always knew. The honey was never
where he thought he'd hidden it, and I hoped the willows
spread their arms over him just as his gold hair
spread around him floating face-down
in Milne's pool. The drowned boy who never dies,
another image in a children's book. You believed
will was enough, that nothing bad
would happen, that our life together would last
if I chose it. I think our choices become us, the way,
outside the house I live in now, the Rose of Sharon,
a weed disguised as a tree, digs in its roots
and blossoms, rising all the way to the second story.
Some day, years from now, one of us
will hear of the death of the other.

# BODIES TERRESTRIAL

*There are also celestial bodies, and bodies terrestrial: but the glory of the celestial
is one, and the glory of the terrestrial is another.*

—I Cor. 15:40

My childhood face floats above fever
and a dream of fever, and all night the ice
has been tapping its message against
the pane. *Sleep, child, sleep. Dream
of your Father in Heaven.* Instead, I drift
in and out of the dream's slow motion,
where skiers ride the air
like angels, their round, startled mouths
opening on nothing. Or a girl spins
and spins until her body blurs, fuses
with the ice. In the black and white film
of the past, snow falls from the stars and settles
in my room, covers the preacher praying
by the bed, touching my forehead
with cold hands. I'm too young to rise up
changed. So that when I think of it
years later, it's like seeing it on a screen,
dim as a documentary in which a skier plunges
headlong down a slope, oblivious
to danger. That's how the young survive, the way
change accumulates like flakes of snow
and means only: this is what happened.
I thought that if I died I would become
a celestial body, according to the Scriptures.
But even in death the body remains
terrestrial. Under the endless stars the dead
spin and spin, and are small.

*for Marsha Recknagel*

## DEAR EVERYONE

How easy it is to sentimentalize
suffering, to love it, as the rabbi said,
more than God does. I don't know why
I remembered this today, what I didn't know

I'd forgotten, thirty years in the past:
In the city with my mother to shop
I'm walking along, oblivious with anticipation,
imagining the Childhoods of Famous Americans arrayed

in their orange bindings on Cokesbury's shelves
and Christmas money in my pocket.
I love these stories in which there is often
poverty, and even death, though children

grow up, despite it all, to do great things
and happiness is reward for virtue. And then I see
the girl—woman, really, but young—walking toward me
down the street. She's dressed in white,

a waitress's uniform maybe, but I don't notice
if she's plain or pretty, I'm so amazed by what
I see. As she walks she's reading a letter and tears
river down her cheeks without a sound. For a moment

there's no sound anywhere, it's like a silent movie,
and I keep looking at her face, which is awash
with grief and pain. She just walks right by and I
turn and stare after her until my mother comes back

to pull me forward. I don't even wonder why
she's crying, though I could invent good reasons.
All I can think of is her face: that I know
something now, know it for the first time and forever—

I will not forget it, though I may forget
the circumstances of its learning—that
there are those who suffer, even unto death,
and are not me, and cannot be consoled.

# THE WATER-BABIES

*But remember . . . this is all a fairy tale . . . and, therefore you are not to believe a word of it even if it is true.*

—Charles Kingsley

In the story by Kingsley the boy
drowns but doesn't die and lives
underwater until he passes
the fairy's tests for manhood and the moral
is Victorian cleanliness and hard work.
Reading it, a child, I thought it happened
because he had no parents there
to save him and a second chance
was possible. Today, watching the children
splashing in the pond, slippery
fishes wriggling in our arms,
I remembered a woman I knew
whose daughter died trick-or-treating
Halloween, darting like a fairy
into the quiet street. The car,
the mother said, came out of nowhere.
I'm a parent now. This is the story I believe.

54

# POEM FOR THE FIRST ANNIVERSARY
# OF MY MOTHER'S DEATH

*Canterbury, Christmas, 1988*

Lost in the crowd pushing
into the Cathedral, we've come so far
from home trying to forget—my father,
my daughter and I—and have to find seats
in the chapel, back behind the choir.
Here only a little sanctuary
is visible from our pew and cold creeps
from the stones. Outside, sheep drowse
in the evergreen fields. In this chapel,
details drift away like incense. I know
the Gospel comes from Luke and the organ
drowns out the choirboys' childish voices.
I can't see from where I sit, but maybe
their parents crane to get a better view,
beaming back at their small sons this moment
of glory. The Archbishop's voice booms
over the loudspeaker. He says today
is full of hope and prays for Lockerbie,
the giant star bursting four days ago
over the sleeping village. He takes heart,
he says, that so much love has poured out
from the nation to all who suffer
and talks of Mrs. Thatcher walking
the smoking wreckage. There's no word
for the wrecked poor suffering alone
in the kingdom's streets. Our tour guide, red
head bowed low, kneels to offer thanks, spared,
for once, by God or luck, her children saved
on an earlier flight. And who am I
to say it wasn't God or that her prayers
don't fly up like doves, rising to flock
with ghosts of all the prayers ever said here?
Maybe even the martyred Becket's prayers
still beat their wings against the vaulted ceiling.
I know there are things I can't understand.
That Wednesday I woke in the dark, caught up
in the net of some vague dream, the clock's
red letters blinking *5:10*. Three hundred miles
away you asked my father to help you
on with your robe, and then you looked surprised,
he said, and fell down on the bathroom floor.

I hated it when he said he asked God
to take you so you wouldn't suffer. But
maybe you asked, maybe you whispered
a prayer in the machine's cold ear
before they unhooked you and let you float
away. When you left my house the morning
after Christmas, I think all you wanted
was to die at home, not like the family
in the pew across from us who want
to go home to their happiness so much
the air shines all around them, like a star.
Say they've just come from opening presents,
and the blond boy leans on his mother's arm,
dreaming of the bicycle he can't wait
to get back to. She bends down and kisses
his hair. Home, then, Father will stoke the fire,
Sister set out the crackers and colored
hats, paper crowns red as holly berries.
Mother will serve them, the table heavy
with food, turkey and potatoes, Christmas
pudding soaked in rum, the tiny mince pies.
Full now, Grandmother dozes in her chair,
the Queen's message winking on the telly.
And here's a last toast to the family
holiday! My father and I won't look
at each other, tied in the knot of the old
quarrel we can't get free from, the way
when he took my arm today to steer me
to the chapel, I shook him off until,
red-faced, he hissed into my ear. He can't
speak of you this season without weeping,
and so we don't. In grief I have become
implacable, single-minded as a tomb.
When the sweet-faced usher comes to take us
to the Eucharist, we shake our heads, stare
straight ahead. Caitlin fidgets, uneasy.
She's nineteen and doesn't know there's nothing
she can do. And then, at last, it's over.
In his gold crown the Archbishop passes
along the aisle, his ruddy, cherubic face
smiling down on his flock, and we
follow, sheep-like, into the overcast noon.
Like an early spring the day

lowers damp and strangely warm.
What does it mean, if it means
anything, weather so out of season?
Imagine the earth warming every year
until we're burning like demons
carved in scenes of Hell, what the sinful
could expect. Imagine my hot cheek pressed
against your hand those hours in the hospital,
as if my body's heat would stop your leaving.

# PINK VISTA

In the dream I carry inside me,
which is no dream, I am always the child
between them. A family sits down to supper,
the yellow kitchen yellow with light.
Father sits here, and Mother sits there, and this chair
in the middle is mine. Someone argues or complains.
Or maybe there is only the drift of talk falling
over us slowly, without sound, like a perfect snow.
I could stop it if I wanted to, with one sweep
send dishes crashing to the floor like God
hurling vengeance at the world, and afterwards
there would be only the absolute and holy
silence of destruction. But I prefer the plate's
pink vista, a landscape where each thing knows
its place: a stream, a stone bridge and beyond them
a house, its roof upturned to the sky.
I will wait there by the door
for my husband the fisherman to bring me
his catch, which I will clean and serve him raw,
with tea and the steaming bowls of rice.
Our child is dead. I bear my grief for him.
I will lay the mats there, side by side.
I will loosen my kimono and cover his face
with kisses, singing to him the legends
of the fathers, the story of the child
who disobeyed the parent and so must swim
forever in the stream beside our house.

# THE BRIDGE TO HEAVEN

When a friend told me, almost
casually, over a meal of carry-out Chinese,
that you were dead, had been for months,
what I felt was not a word for being
surprised by something bad, banal
in its easy, spendthrift horror. What I felt
was the shock of a current suddenly shot
through the body, so that the chopsticks flew
from my hands. For a moment I thought
I saw your face there in a Blue Willow
plate, in the water drifting so quietly
under the bridge, then hidden somewhere deep
among the trees. But when I shook myself
awake, your death seemed to me like one
written in a fortune cookie, foreign
and incomprehensible, a tasteless joke.
That's how we improvise
grief, one moment to the next.

What I feel now is not just grief
but guilt. Guilt for not keeping in touch,
not answering your letter, for somehow
not knowing you were gone, and more,
for my fear of your fear, your need
too like my own. That summer in California,
both of us away from home, we met
across our poems, our sadness. You worried
your choices on your slender fingers
like a worn rosary, none of them
without sorrow. You couldn't bring yourself
to leave for good. Years before,
I'd left a family—two children
younger than yours, a husband—and grief
settled in me the way poison oak hides
in the green foothills. I kept my distance
and wouldn't touch it. When your young lover
came to visit, he bounded into the room
and swept you up, making you blush.
The next day your husband came.
Nervous and blustering, he laid his hand
on your shoulder as though to hold you
firmly to the earth, as though
you might fly away. I know that

seems too obvious, and yet, maybe
that's what we all want, something
common as a lovers' triangle, but strange
to us, a moment so clear and impossible
it lifts us above our mundane lives
until we ourselves become a poem.

I keep imagining you as you come home
that night, flushed, maybe, with wine,
walking into the garage and seeing
your husband working among his tools,
nails bright as money, the saws
with their sharp teeth laid out
on the wooden table. Maybe your mind
is on a poem you'd started
that morning, how you might end it.
The moment he turns and fires
the gun your eyes open wide
with surprise. (An accident, he says,
so grief-stricken he has to be
carried from your funeral. But your friends
don't believe him, and your children
are divided. Soon he will marry again.)
It's true you looked at the world
like that. Even beauty surprised you,
even the black and blue bird, Steller's jay,
hovering on the deck, so expectant
of the breadcrumbs you'd offer he'd wait
and wait. You said he looked "like a man
who's gone swimming with his hat on."
And sometimes you did seem about to fly up,
not like the jay, satisfied at last,
but startled, like a dove flushed
from the underbrush who hears the hunter's
heavy boots crackling the dry grass.

Mornings you passed my window
with the notebook you carried everywhere
for poems and disappeared for hours.
Later, I learned where you went.
The day you left for home, you led me miles
across the pasture, over fence after fence,
past piles of cow dung rotting in the sun,

to show me what you'd found. Through a grove
of eucalyptus, their faint funereal odor,
beyond the leering, twisted madrone
you called The Naked Man Tree, the redwoods
blocked out the light. Only a weak shaft
fell on the waterfall and the still pool
thick with ferns, the dark place
where a girl had drowned herself, sick
with longing. We sat for a long time
on the moss-covered ground, listening
to water rush over the stones, like tears
of grief that fall and fall and will not
stop. You wept then, too, and I wished
I had something to give you, some consolation,
like the evening we climbed a hill
near Half Moon Bay and watched the fog's
purple script drift along the coast.
Skywriting, I said, and pointed out to you,
delicate as calligraphy, an oriental city
traced on the dusky sky. Above our heads,
a pagoda, lacy fans, a willow tree, and higher
still, farther out above the horizon,
the curved bridge that leads to Heaven.

*for A. N., in memory*

# THE FAMILY TABLE

Old hurts aren't forgotten exactly—
what your brother did to you or you
to him, who got the most marbles, the most
love. Time doesn't heal all wounds,
but sometimes it covers them like layers
of skin, the way you have to look hard
to see the faint scar on your knee
where you fell through the rotten porch
thirty years ago. And so tonight the father
who seemed to love the world more
than you tells how he spent all day
with his grandson, showing the child over and over
how to hammer a nail into pine and the delight
of mastery when he got it right. In the future
your number will diminish one
by one, but you imagine the children's
children filling the table and tonight
there is good food and good talk, talk
of how many blueberries each child picked today,
of rebels in Nicaragua, of swimming and a protest
at a nuclear plant. In every story there is
a stranger at the door, a cancer blooming deep
in the chest, a scorpion crouched
amid fragrant boughs of pine, but sometimes
there is also a crisp Chardonnay
and on the blue plate the red claws
yield to the touch, the meat
plucked out and dipped in lemony butter.
And afterwards there will be blueberries
that float in cream and stain
our lips and beards with juice.
*Dessert,* we say, because we all deserve
some sweetness in the end.

*for Peter Brown*

# NOTES

"Birthright"—Ken Millar, that mild, sad man, was known to the world as Ross Macdonald, creator of Lew Archer and author of an acclaimed series of novels that are as much family romances as they are detective stories. He died of Alzheimer's disease in 1983. Some of the details in this poem are based on events in his life.

"Distances"—Brian Jones, one of the original members of the Rolling Stones, lived at Cotchford Farm, the former estate of his favorite writer, A. A. Milne, author of *Winnie-the-Pooh,* a book Jones was said to know "by heart." Because of his heavy use of drugs, Jones was asked to leave the Stones early in the summer of 1969. On July 2, he was found drowned in his swimming pool.